Still Life With Octopus

Still Life With Octopus

Tania Hershman

Nine
Arches
Press

Still Life With Octopus
Tania Hershman

ISBN: 978-1-913437-42-8
eISBN: 978-1-913437-43-5

First published July 2022 by:

Nine Arches Press
Unit 14, Sir Frank Whittle Business Centre,
Great Central Way, Rugby.
CV21 3XH
United Kingdom

www.ninearchespress.com

Printed in the United Kingdom by:
Imprint Digital

Nine Arches Press is supported using public funding by Arts Council England.

Contents

"To completely forgo both skeleton and shell is an unusual evolutionary move for a creature of this size and complexity. An octopus has almost no hard parts at all – its eyes and beak are the largest – and as a result can squeeze through a hole about the size of its eyeball and transform its body shape almost indefinitely. The evolution of cephalopods yielded, in the octopus, a body of pure possibility."

– Peter Godfrey Smith, *Other Minds: The Octopus and the Evolution of Intelligent Life*

Arrival

What if you didn't know
        what *night* was, landing here.
What if you'd never heard
        of *light*. Which words
would you use to describe
        this, with no *dark*, no *shadows*,
stars. And if you stayed
        long enough, how would the shift
to *day* be, with everything
        you hadn't known was there
                appearing
                        like a *ship*, a *shock*, a *bird*;
                          or like every bird at once,
                            flying at you, *singing*.

Still Life With Octopus (I)

There is an octopus in my chest, trying
to give my heart to you. She will not listen

when I say I need it. I have to keep
prying her from my vena cava, the pulmonary

veins. I ask what makes her think
you'd want it anyway. She shakes her head, her colour

shifts to indicate disappointment, hope,
connection. Finally, I let her take it. Once

it's gone, she settles in its place, exactly the right
cardiac muscle shade. I worry about where my heart

is now, did it even reach you? Let go, whispers the octopus
in my chest. These things are not in your control.

What You May Be Offered

A man in a van stopped to ask
if I wanted a mattress. I said

no. I was sitting drinking tea
by the river. How did he think

I'd get it home? He was on his way back,
he said, from a mattress show. What

was it about me, sitting by the river,
drinking tea, that made him think this

was what I needed? I am
here again today, by the river

with my tea, wondering
what someone might offer me.

Fed

I say to the chef
Make me something
with cheese. The chef

is my mother, my father,
my uncles and aunts,
the grandmothers

I never had. Wait
by the sea, says the chef,

so I sit in the waves
and I wave at the shells

and I shell up my heart
and I hearten my feet

with a fork in my hand,
and a spoon on my tongue.
Not long now, says the chef. Not long.

Grip

On a Dublin street, I pass
a man who makes as if
to shield his heart from me. But I

am not a threat in that
department, theft
of breath or vital organs has never

been my plan. Maybe I'm wrong. Maybe
there is something precious – not blood
or meat or muscle – in his inside

jacket pocket he was trying
to protect. You walked so
quickly, I didn't see your face, might

have recognised
one who also slips
out in the world. Hold on.

Making New

This is new to me, this setting of a boundary, new to my heart, walking dark. The night is comforting, I let go of everything I cannot see. You.

I cannot see you. I let go of comforting. Everything is night, my heart a walking boundary. This new setting of me is dark.

I am setting my heart new, you cannot see this dark boundary, this everything. Walking is comforting. I let go.

I am comforting me. This new boundary, my heart, cannot dark. Let go the night, everything I see is new.

Territorial Disputes

I will not claim you even if
you say I can even if

you want me to You are
no moon I have no flag I will not

fix myself to you in public
so everyone might see You are

not mine even if
you want to be whisper

I am yours *completely* I know
how this works The surface

of the moon

is never smooth

I am

part-leaf
	part-lake

and if you
	want me

to float
	and weave

skim air
	and take in

currents, I
	will be

the lawns
	your feet

slide along
	the bank

you can
	never reach.

Catherine the Great Reassesses her Expansionist Policies

I am Catherine the Great
and I seize this jetty, this
is my section of the lake. These

are my ducks, I claim
all reeds. I declare
vertical dominion: if you want

to use my airspace, pay me. Where is
my army? Just one
phone call away. They say I

am an enlightened
despot, so I'll teach
the ducks to read, the reeds

to sing. And I will
bring my lover here,
although she won't speak, there

is too much
talking in my portion
of the lake. You ask

why am I content
with part, why not take it
all? Child, you too will learn

that happiness
never comes
from having more of anything.

Uncertainty

It is the only bird
which does this
(that we know of,
that we've seen).

But, then again, it is
the only bird
that spends so much
time in the air
(weeks, we reckon
from our measuring).

And one of the only
seabirds (that we know of,
that we've seen)
which failed to insist

on wings with proper
waterproofing. So the frigate bird
uses clouds as rest-stops, as
an elevator. What goes on

between bird and cloud
is not clear (from our
measuring). We are also
unsure (given the current

limits on our instruments)
how the cloud might benefit
from this arrangement.

By the River

The geese are meeting to discuss the fog, or
to discuss how anyone can play golf
in this weather. Golfing men, it seems

are not put off by a disappearing ball, invisible
tee, which tells you something about the game
of golf, or men perhaps. I have been released

after a week of weakness, and everything –
the geese, the golfing men, ducks, joggers, dogs –
is sweet to me. Through the haze, I notice

the outline of a man with clubs approach the geese
and wonder if he is cajoling, offering or asking
for permission. And then for an instant

the fog lifts, and I see man, clubs and geese moving
in harmony. I watch the dance until I cannot tell
who is who or what, and when the curtain drops, I

walk on knowing
no-one, not even you,
will believe me.

It was the Epoch

It was the epoch of the shoeless saleswomen. We'd watch them saunter down our street. Before they started work we'd see them paint each other's toes, each day a different colour. The shoeless saleswomen laughed and painted, and how we wanted to grow up to be them! But now is the age of the heavy-booted marketing exec. We do not reach down in the morning to cup our colleague's foot, turn her nails turquoise. Our boots stay on so long we are not sure we still have anything inside. At night we dream of crimson lacquer, of base and top coats, of the saleswomen's gentle arches, how they softly swooped to bring us everything we ever wanted.

Still Life With Octopus (II)

I only asked her once to climb inside a jar for me. (Before we met, I'd watched all the videos of those experiments.) She sighed but did it, said I could screw the lid, released herself easily. You could become any shape you want, I said. She said nothing. One arm sent itself out to switch the kettle on. While she made us tea, I put the jar back in the cupboard, feeling that slight ache from too much sitting in my hip bones, my lower back, where fixed part meets fixed part of me.

Nevermuch

Everything has become
                              too much and I thought

there was not enough
                              of it. Everything

has become too much and I
                              am not enough

of it. Every thought
                              I have

becomes too much and too
                              enough of me for it.

I am all my thought and think
                              too much, because

of you, who is too
                              much, never enough.

What Plays Today

Between my ears:
a radio. I choose

the station. Sometimes
the dial sticks. Sometimes

static or the sound
of someone softly screaming.

Standardized Patient

Today I am your
lower back pain. Listen,
I have all the details, will
not veer

from the script. Tomorrow
I will be your cancer
of the kidneys. Next week,

I may be your
one-legged skier (I know,
I know). Whose pain
is this?

Note: **Standardized patient simulation** lets medical students practice on people trained to play patients.

And a Clock

It was not truly
a thunderstorm, that awful
ghost lighting, those
small crashes, out
of the corner of your eye
weather
or a dream

of weather. And in the
dream, a tree is
coming in, dark
and mossy. And in the dream
the tree
is asking, Tell me who

this *me* is. You try
to answer but your mouth
is filled with feathers
and a clock
that ticks just once
an hour.

And then God

sends someone else's
Jewish grandmother
to stop me

with a question about birds
I can't answer. She says – as if
this is her river – I've never

seen you here before,
then presses for my
exact address. Instead

of the usual, Such a nice
girl, no husband?, she asks,
No dog? I don't know why

I tell her then
that I'm a poet, but
the gleam in her eyes

warns me this
is the point
to leave, the unasked

dancing on the path
between us: Will you
make a poem out of me?

Still Life With Octopus (III)

My octopus – three hearts, eight semi-independent arms – can never choose just one book to read, skims several, gets the plots confused, although arm five has a good grasp of a novel, while her brain is wrapping itself around *Best American Science and Nature Writing,* and I wonder how all this goes on at once without a centre where the story sits.

Psalm for the Seamstresses

After Carl Sandburg

The seamstresses know each feel of cotton, silk and wool. Their hands are maps of effort. Their eyes are used to dimness. The seamstresses laugh while sewing, pour each other tea and coffee. They prefer their needles sharp, their voices low, every stitch next to its sisters. If they bleed, they bleed. The seamstresses start with pieces, end with objects. At day's close they fold and wrap. No-one can undo what they have created.

Tied

She lives when women
are tied tight, are
unvoiced, unpublic, when

the men have swords,
have shouting, and horses
own the roads. She lives

when there is a king
who marries and re-
marries, while she sits,

unchilded, unattached,
at home, a disappointment
to her parents. She keeps

her hands floured,
there are always
crumbs of something in

her hair, her elbows, and
in the corner of
each eye. She rarely thinks

of the king, never
wonders which
wife he is trying

to free himself from
now. She takes
her bread out

of the oven, sits
and waits
for it to cool.

When the Time Comes

Caesar says this

is the place, so I tie it

with string and the dune

sees me work, with sand

in my hand, and I stop

and I start and the dune

and the clouds, and I make myself

new, all the cities unbuilt

when the time comes to sing, I will know

if the sky is untied.

Application

When she goes for
the position they will
ask her: Are you familiar

with your inner organs: liver,
lungs, the heart? The almost-mother
will not answer, never having

had any training from
her own (or largely silent
father) to reach inside. As they

discuss her after the interview, all
agree she doesn't tick
the boxes. The almost-father, too,

scores badly. The recommendation
is that neither undertake this kind
of role, it would cause frustration,

disappointment, no chance
of harmony, of teamwork or
promotion. As she waits, the almost-

mother picks up a magazine
from the table. "Want to be the perfect
parent!" screams the cover. She finds

a pen, answers the questions, but,
knowing already which section
her points total will place her in,

doesn't finish reading. You might
be okay, says her heart. There's room
for improvement, say her lungs. The liver

claps and nods. But the almost-mother
sits, oblivious, hearing nothing, not knowing
how to listen.

Middle of the Night

Night asks me
to wake up. What?
I say. Night whispers
darkly, something
about cats coming in
and out, a baby five
doors down. You
want company? I ask.
Night nods. I get up

and we make tea. Too
early, the cat mutters
as we pass. Night
and I get back
into bed. I'm fine
now, Night says.

Tango

Mother, take your daughter
dancing. Invite her

to tango. I know
it sounds unusual

but you'll find
many others

on the floor. You might
waltz, if you prefer,

you don't have to
touch her, there

are different ways
to move. Every now

and then, though, stop,
smile, tap

her elbow, reel
her in.

Still Life With Octopus (IV)

My octopus introduces me to her friend. A saltwater crocodile, she tells me. Look at that skull, I say, what a magnificent head. I am a bit jealous, says my octopus, of the power of her jaw, given that I have no bones at all. Her friend takes all our compliments in silence, just a nod. She isn't chatty, says my octopus, that's why we get on. I understand, I say, and since they seem to want to be alone, put down the tea tray. As I leave, I hear the crocodile murmur, What do you see in her? She's like an alien, says my octopus, so fascinating.

The Aunts

After Maria Pawlikowska-Jasnorzewska

Goodness and badness, stray from them
equally, say the aunts, robust
as hens and tough as millet seeds. Some

look through the window, others
are solving puzzles in a corner, one
is painting my ceiling. Good

and bad? I say. The aunts shake
and nod their heads. Outside
is a bird I've never seen before. But

isn't it better to be good? The aunts
reach out their arms until I am inside
a circle of them. They are smiling,

angry. You will bend, they say,
for kindness, for charity, you will
break. And badness, too, will split you,

you will drown in air. Every aunt
is standing, every aunt is whispering
behind my eyes. Aim for the centre,

child, be middling, average,
fair. Laughing, they let me go.
The painter picks up her brush. One

puzzle-solving aunt points out
a bare spot on the ceiling. I stare
and stare, but just can't see it.

Resignation

If there's only one
family per life that you
emerge from, no

possibility of swapping
some or all of them

for one or more
    who listen
one or more
    who see further

than child, sister,
then may I, fifty one

years later, tender
my resignation, pass

the position to someone
more qualified? Please

address all correspondence
to a small island, no map

provided, and no guarantee
that anyone will ever reach me.

My Moon

I planned to report it
to the owner of the building opposite, found
his name, his number, planned

to say, Do you know
that the hall light on your top floor
goes on and off all day

and night, say it kindly, as if
I was concerned not about
the dazzling of my bedroom

window, but his expenses, his
electric bill. I never
got around to it, and now

a year or so later, find myself
fond of this ever-watching,
ever-watchful artificial moon. We nod

to each other as I sit in bed. My moon –
those living in the building itself
can't see her from their flats, although I suppose

someone in the house across from me
might claim her too – who I thought once
so nosy, always shining in

too bright, I now see as interested,
curious. What are you
writing? she asks. Is it about

me? I grin at her this Saturday, my
day of recovery, too many people –
builders – in my house all week, so much

noise, unpredictability. My moon
is constant, powered, untidal, she doesn't
pull me, doesn't ask for anything. Do you

mind, I say, if I am? Ha, says the moon,
which is perhaps a laugh. Now, she says,
I can compete a little with that

other one, who only comes at dark, the one
everybody sings about. No competition,
I say. Different, that's all. You're no shape-

shifter, no-one takes a rocket
out to map you, name
your parts. True, she says. Even you

can't come closer, won't see
me. I see you, I say, what else
is this poem? True again,

says my moon. We sit quietly,
the cat, the moon and I, remind each other
how to shine.

Time

breaks off its course, seconds
pile up
like chocolate
coins. Three hours
come at once. You sigh
at the end of a day
stacked with several,
overlapping. You lose
sight of where, of when, then
and now, and, dizzy,
are relieved. You catch
a nanosecond in your teeth,
for longer
than you should.

Over, Forwards, Back

She does not expect
to come upon her name, right there
on the first street she tiptoes
down after leaving

the machine. Five centuries
back, four countries over,
and there it is, unusual
or maybe not, on a post

hammered beside
a gate. The house
is empty. She looks
through the window

for great-great-grand-
parents, some distant
cousin, anyone. But all
she sees is a cloth

on the floor, a small
carpet she thinks
she recognises. Later,

in the machine, going
over, forwards, back,
she cries.

A Hierarchy of Arms

From observations, we believe
an octopus's arms to be

semi-autonomous. We cannot
be certain, we disagree. Some say

its arms act only when
authorised. Some say, *What proof*

do you have, and then
we fight. Politely,

in our own language,
in journal papers and

at conferences. One or other
of us floats one

or more outlandish theories:
the arms are separate

creatures, barely attached,
parasites. Or: the body keeps

some arms on a tight leash,
charged with movement, hiding,

foraging; the others explore,
gather data. To test this

we trap octopuses, affix
our probes. They rip them

off. At night, after they think
we've gone, we wait behind

the laboratory door,
and although none of us

ever speaks of it, we are fairly sure
we hear them laughing.

How to Make a Buttonhole Hand Stitch, 3 minutes 15 seconds, Feb 21, 2018

// You only see her hands / She doesn't speak / doesn't say / as they all do / Today I'm going to show you how / She sews / for three minutes fifteen seconds / in silence/ But there is noise / Behind her / dogs are barking / children shout / at one point there's a siren / the sound of drilling / Because you have nothing but her fingers / (nails shaped but not quite clean) / you imagine / Some city in America / (sirens, dogs) / A woman who has told her family / Don't bother me / I'm filming / And for three minutes fifteen seconds / she unlistens / to the children / dogs / sirens / drill / till she finishes that buttonhole for you //

I'm in charge

of no-one
but myself. She

is not always
obedient.

Sfat Em

Mother's tongue

I have to leave
the language in which –

by what she says
or by her silence –

I am never right. I
choose another, begin

myself again
inside it. Years

later, after I've been
re-made in words

from right to left, I feel
safe to come

back to the first.
But now, with this

unsafety in and out, I
am drawn to that other

direction, the other
tongue. How odd –

or maybe not – that
the one I picked fits

my body best. There is
no-one here to speak it

with. It was never that.
I sing it to myself.

To John Clare, May 2020

Dear John, I am interested
in your interest
in insects, the city
of black ants you
are peering at
under that tree, their
government, their
community. What
language do you
imagine they speak
whisperingly? I too

have written
about insects' sense
of togetherness. Do you
know the fire ant? It's almost
indestructible, in groups
they form bridges,
rafts, to overcome
disaster. I am interested

in your choice
of insect names: tiny
loiterers, happy
units, things
of mind. Fairies. Is it
their size that sets you
to see them magically, or
something else
about their industry,
the complete worlds
beneath our eyeline? I hear

despair in your talk
of a fly's liberty
to creep, to be
as it likes. Seldom,
you write, do they do
wrong. You are too
hard on yourself,
John. We all
do wrong
and right and everything
between. It's nature. I'm sure

a fly, an ant,
seeing us, would
wonder, too, at how
we think, attempt and plan,
what we create, what we
unmake, the dark
and bright magic that we do.

Still Life With Octopus (V)

Today my octopus has eight umbrellas. Are we expecting friends? I say. I am setting up a stall, she says. Some think the rain will never end. Clever, I say, and together we put up the table. She is so much faster than me, I stop and watch, often it's a blur. Do you miss the water? I ask. She raises two arms to the sky. We both look up, drops falling in our eyes. I get it, I say. We sell all our umbrellas that first day. The octopus treats me to cake, indoors. We watch the rain slip down the window. There is nowhere, she says, that I would rather be.

Being Wrong

Go on a walk
with corners. Take off

your glasses, slip,
laughing. Let the river

fool you. Watch each bend
produce a jogger, whisper

I know, I know. You'd think,
said the man in the cafe

to his friend, we'd agree
on what colour red is. Mistake

all of it for everything.

Play

says the girl in the coat
by the piano, who knows

I only sat down
by accident, haven't

the skills to do
what she wants

on the black
and the white of it. Put

your hands here,
says the girl with the coat

by the piano, placing hers
over mine on the cool

and the dark of it, whispering
notes in my ear.

You Blow Me Away

When we meet, I have
all my armour, by which
I mean: my skin

and everything below. You
flay me slowly, love,
saying, Let go. Let it all

go. I find myself difficult
to unpin, but, like a knight
returning from her final joust,

eventually I lay aside
my battledress, stand
naked on your hill,

every nut
and every bolt
of me exposed.

On the 111 Bus

I sit next to someone
else's grandmother on the
one-eleven into town. She'd sat
down next to me, my favourite seat,
top deck, front, when I wanted

to be alone. The bus isn't
crowded, she chose me, it
seems, and as we get
to that point of a sharp left
turn, before the roundabout, I see her

dive into her shopping bag. For a moment
I imagine she might have a hat stand
in there, or a ladder she'd draw out, rung
by rung. Instead, it is

Tupperware. She takes off the lid, turns,
offers me one. Macaroons, says
someone else's grandmother. I look
at her for the first time, as the bus goes
past the playing fields. Why me? I want

to ask, but don't. I reach
in, take a biscuit. Neither of us
smiles. Thank you, I say, and desperately
want to get up, go down, get off. I sit there
holding the macaroon. The next stop

without a word, she leaves me. A few
days later, I will find the macaroon
in my pocket, will take a moment
to remember, hesitate, then slip it
in my mouth.

Learning to be Good

After Tony Hoagland

The good people
take turns giving
the rest of us lessons
in it. Each one has a slightly
different style
of handout. Some
of them are better
at picking fonts. The good
people don't get irritated
with those of us who
never know what page
to turn to. Or, if they do,
they only discuss it later,
amongst themselves.

What We Choose To Call You

At the Manchester Museum

And I am thinking of you,
litoria splendida, the Australian
Splendid Tree Frog. I am thinking

of coming across you
after all those rooms
of parts and lifelessness

> five grey goose wings, the owl heads
> and feet, that porcupine,
> the shells and molluscs

that men collected
on expeditions. I am
remembering

what joy to turn
the corner and there
was life! In a case

intended for a green tree
snake, above some apology, but
who could apologise

for you, one behind the other
on that leaf, blinking
at me. Oh splendid tree frogs,

do you know what we
have called you? Would it be
a weight, the awareness

that you are named
for your magnificence? Curious,
I discover other splendids –

> a cicada, several moths, a butterfly, ant, fungus,
> yellow loach fish, land snail, the tabar pitta bird,
> an orchid, and oh my, the *Bolitoglossa splendida* salamander.

You could have a splendid
gathering, a party! But

one of you might snack
on another, or fight

over who is the most... No. Stay
on your leaf, you have

nothing left to prove. I go,
feeling myself splendid
for having turned that corner,

stumbled on you, but by the time
I get down all the stairs
and through the gift shop

to the street, I feel
ordinary, one part
of the flow. At home,

I think how glad I am
not to be invited
to any splendid party,

all that squabbling. I sit
on my own leaf, choose
my label, my display

case. Maybe, dear frogs,
when I come back,
you will tell me
what your true name is.

I have put so many things down

Some I have let drop
Some I have set on the ground by my feet
Some I have thrown as far as possible

I carried so much my arms were fixed in that shape
I carried so much my muscles had not moved for decades

When I began
to put things down
to drop things
to throw them away
my arms began to soften
When I began not to
carry everything
my muscles sang

The things I dropped are broken
The things I threw away are gone
Those by my feet may be picked up again

I want to put you down
You are fine, beautiful and
heavy as a planet
            I bend a knee
            I try to set you by my feet
            but my arm
my arm
            will not release you yet

Still Life With Octopus (VI)

Between the octopus and her arms

is an agreement: arm will wander, touch,

explore, report some of its findings back, but

no obligation. Each arm may keep things to itself – how it felt

to stroke the metal remnant

of that hull, what it found

behind the furthest

shell. And the body, too,

has things it will never tell.

I am interested

in myself. Sometimes
I examine my hands as if
they belonged to someone else.
I watch the fingers move, ripples of
skin, the wrinkles that appear. I am interested in
my limbs, the miracle of forearm, a mole, the soft side
of the neck. I cut my own hair by feeling edge and curl. I am
interested in the age of me, notice changes in my shift, my spin. I
am interested in breath, in breathing, in what I lose, in all that I take in.

When I empty to space

completely, my left ankle
vanishes. I hadn't meant
for it to go. I slide
my fingers round the ankle-
space and wonder
what might leave me

next. It troubles me
less than I would have
thought, and in fact, later on,
for balance, dismiss the other
ankle too. When there is a call

to bring the beautiful
back into our lives, I don't
ask my ankles home. They
weren't beautiful
to me, I realise. I start

to examine my wayward
hips, my pylon elbows.
Finally, I rest on my knees
as the part I most admire,
the jointedness,
the bearing of such
loads. You are gorgeous,

I whisper to each knee cap, and
to be generous, praise
my shoulders, cheeks, the ends
of my short short hair, my
fingertips. I understand

they are right, the movement
for beauty inclusion: once
I begin, I see something
wonderful in all my parts,
including thyroid gland,
frontal lobe, appendix. I ask

my ankles for forgiveness
that I dismissed them so
quickly. I shut
my delicious eyes, wait for
the ankle-spaces
to fill up again, with bone
and flesh, toes and
almost-arch. Welcome.

And in the arrangement of salt

with pepper,
teapot, cup and saucer, water
bottle with its curl
of cucumber, glasses
drunk from, menu

And in the arrangement
of mother with daughter,
husband and wife, dog
or cat with its curl
of tail, beds
slept in, a house

And in the arrangement
of salt with wife,
cat and daughter, saucer, husband
with no curl

And the table: reset

And the flowers refreshed,
salt and pepper filled

And the woman before
mother/wife

And the husband, tea-
pot, cup and saucers

Salt the woman, pepper
her unchildren, curl
the unbecoming husband, refill
the dog, leave the water
bottle out, sit down
at the unwiped table, push
your cup, lick the menu clean. You can order
everything.

And then everything

becomes

a way

to tell

yourself

I am doing fine
I am doing fine

Still Life With Octopus (VII)

And what if the octopus could talk.
And what if they turned to us and said, Enough
with all the jars, the tests of what we
can get into and get through. You've seen
what we can do.

What if, instead, they took us
in their arms, said, We've been watching
too. We've seen what you get yourselves
into, what you're struggling

to get through. Let us help you
see your jars, your lids, let us teach you to
loosen
          breathe
                    undo

Arrival

put me down
until I lift me

put me aside
until I lean

put me out
until I dessicate

put me under
until I drown

put me over
until I'm rolled up tight

put me back
until I come

put me high
until I slowly sink

put me home
and we are done

Notes

Still Life With Octopus (I): An octopus's skin has cells called chromatophores which allow them to change the colour, sometimes for camouflage, to blend in with their surroundings, sometimes for reasons we don't understand at all. Turning the same colour as the cardiac muscle should be possible, although an octopus has not yet, that we know of, replaced a human heart.

Still Life With Octopus (II): Scientists spend a lot of time capturing octopuses and making them escape from inside jars with the lids screwed on. The octopus finds this pretty easy. (You can watch the videos on the Octolab YouTube Octopus Escapes channel: https://www.youtube.com/playlist?list=PL8KV6JJhlaOmvvyO6aIae53abFtDV_NPT)

Still Life With Octopus (III) and A Hierarchy of Arms: No-one's really sure what the relationship is between an octopus and her arms, just that the arms not only have neurons, they have "twice as many as in the central brain" (Other Minds, Peter Godfrey-Smith). Who knows who is really in charge of who?

Still Life With Octopus (IV): An octopus has no bones, in fact she has no hard parts to her body at all. This is how an octopus can get herself in and out of even the tiniest spaces and recreate herself in many different shapes.

The Aunts: This poem was commissioned for the Manchester Polish Poetry Festival 2018 to celebrate renowned Polish poet Maria Pawlikowska-Jasnorzewska, who is buried in Manchester's Southern Cemetery. The following lines were taken from her poems as translated by Barbara Bogoczek & Tony Howard (https://maria-pawlikowska-jasnorzewska.com/love). "Robust as hens and tough as millet seeds," from 'Aunts'; "goodness and badness, stray from them equally" from 'Whoever wants me to love him'; "drowns in air" from 'A Letter'.

How to Make a Buttonhole Hand Stitch, 3 minutes 15 seconds, Feb 21, 2018: https://www.youtube.com/watch?v=vWxjg3JUzIM

Dear John: This poem was commissioned as a response to the work of English Romantic nineteenth-century poet John Clare for The Thunder Mutters, a poetry and music podcast by Adam Horovitz and Becky Dallow, and broadcast in 2020. My poem includes quotes from the following Clare poems: 'Insects' and 'House or Window Flies'.

You Blow Me Away: This poem was inspired by 'You Blew Me Away 8', an outdoor sculpture by Penny Hardy. You can see a photograph of it here: http://www.pennyhardysculpture.com/index.aspx?sectionid=1204432blew

What We Choose to Call You: This began life as an audio poem commissioned by First Draft Manchester to respond to a work in a museum. It was inspired by the Australian Splendid Tree Frogs I came upon in the Manchester Museum.

Acknowledgements

Thank you to Peter Godfrey-Smith, whose wonderful book, *Other Minds: The Octopus and the Evolution of Intelligent Life* (William Collins, 2017), set my own mind spinning, kick-starting a fascination with octopuses that I never imagined would evolve into the poems here.

Thank you to Ann and Peter Sampson of the Poetry Business and all the members of the 2019-2020 Poetry Business Writing School, where many of these poems were born, including the first 'Still Life With Octopus' poems.

Thank you to Helen Eastman and Live Canon for selecting my poetry pamphlet, *How High Did She Fly?*, as joint winner of the 2019 poetry pamphlet competition. A number of poems from the pamphlet are included here.

Thank you to the editors of the literary magazines where versions of a number of these poems were first published: *Butcher's Dog* ('Tied'); *Finished Creatures* ('By The River', 'Nevermuch'); *The Pickled Body* ('What You Might Be Offered'); The Rialto ('Grip'); Verve Poetry Competition Anthology 2022 ('And in the arrangement of salt'), *Impossible Archetype* ('Still Life with Octopus (I)'). Thank you to Katrina Naomi for commending my poem, 'How To Make A Buttonhole Hand Stitch, 3 Minutes 15 seconds, Feb 21, 2018', in the 2022 Poetry Teignmouth competition.

Thank you to Ian McMillan and Faith Lawrence and everyone at Radio 3's *The Verb* for inviting me on their octopus-themed programme in June 2020 to read several of my poems alongside Peter Godfrey-Smith, the author of the book which inspired them!

Thank you to all the Barmooristas – Chris, Jo, Lesley, Matt, Nell, Robbie, Rosie, Sarah, and Sean – whose inspiration, support and most excellent company on our North Yorkshire writing retreats helped bring forth and put a shine on many of these poems.